THE
BEATLES

THE
BEATLES

BY THE
EDITORS OF
LIFE

A Bulfinch Press Book
Little, Brown and Company
Boston • New York • Toronto • London

Edited by Robert Friedman
Photo-edited by David Friend
Designed by Tom Bentkowski and Mimi Park
Written by Charles Hirshberg

Staff: Melanie deForest, Gail Ridgwell, Pamela Sztybel Winningham (photo research);
Allison Adato, Jen M.R. Doman, Joshua R. Simon (reporting);
Robert Sullivan (editing); Harriet Barovick, Kerry Candaele (research);
Robert Andreas, Hilary Handelsman, Larry Nesbitt (copy);
Lawrence P. Bracken (editorial production)

Album covers on page 97 courtesy of
Danny Prisco of Danny's Records,
110 W. 25th St., New York, N.Y.,
Danny D'Antonio and Mark Lapidos

Shea Stadium ticket on page 72 and button on page 128
from the collection of Jeff Augsburger

Photographs on pages 2, 42, 48 from It Was Thirty Years Ago Today. Copyright © 1994
by Terence Spencer. Excerpted by arrangement with
Henry Holt & Company, Inc. (U.S.) and Bloomsbury Publishing Ltd. (U.K.).
Photograph on page 40 reprinted with permission from Bloomsbury Publishing Ltd.

HARRY BENSON

First Edition

ISBN 0-8212-2317-8

Library of Congress Catalog Card Number 96-83224

A CIP catalogue record for this book is
available from the British Library

Published simultaneously in the United States of America
by Bulfinch Press, an imprint and trademark
of Little, Brown and Company (Inc.), in Great Britain
by Little, Brown and Company (UK) Ltd., and
in Canada by Little, Brown & Company (Canada) Limited

PRINTED IN THE UNITED STATES OF AMERICA

LINDA MCCARTNEY

Remember

One night early in 1964, I was sitting in a London jazz club called Ronnie Scott's when three of the Beatles walked in—John Lennon, George Harrison and Ringo Starr. They looked like aliens.

Ronnie Scott's in those lost days was a stark and toxic basement in Chinatown, packed sardine-tight with England's idea of hipsters. Jazz cool meant sharkskin suits and short hair, razor-sharp trouser creases, impenetrable dark glasses—the Bobby Darin look from *Too Late Blues*. It also meant a studious austerity. Few words, fewer gestures and no trace of emotion ever. And suddenly here came the Beatles, all flash and furor, with their long hair flapping, their velvet-collared jackets and high-heeled Chelsea boots.

by Nik Cohn
photography by Harry Benson

They were already the Fab Four, all the rage in Britain. "She Loves You" and "I Want to Hold Your Hand" had changed both the sound and the attitude of English pop forever. But they hadn't yet invaded America, and their success was still on a human scale. Any thought of them as godheads or generational icons would have been laughable. On this night they seemed nothing more than the latest teen idols—"the pimple of the month," as the *Daily Mirror* put it—and the prevailing wisdom was that they wouldn't last.

If the Beatles felt pressured, however, they certainly didn't show it. Ringo's hands flashed gold rings, Lennon laughed with his mouth open wide, and all three seemed to speak in code, the thick Scouse patois of Liverpool that barred all outsiders. Across the tiny room, the great Dexter Gordon was playing tenor sax, but they gave no sign of hearing him. Just stood by themselves at the bar, racketing, while all the hipsters stared, pretending not to.

Such arrogance, such a total self-reliance—it seemed indecent somehow. To be so young and so utterly without doubt. They took one drink and then departed in the middle of a number. When they left, it felt as if every breath of air went with them.

Dexter Gordon's set ended, the crowd dispersed. Inside the club, jazzmen clustered round the bar, darkly muttering. Most of them referred to the Beatles' visit only in obscenities, but one, a globular man named Tubby Hayes, seemed more baffled than irate. He kept shaking his chins, as if at a great mystery. "All I want to know," he said, "is *Why?*"

It seemed a fair question at the time, and it still seems relevant now. At first glance, the Beatles hardly looked like world-beaters. They wrote catchy tunes, they had vitality and freshness, they were quirkily attractive, and they gave snappy answers in interviews. On the other hand, they were never highly regarded as a live band, certainly not by their peers, and the cloned outfits that Brian Epstein insisted they wear were hopelessly tacky. Superficially, there was no overwhelming reason they should outrank the Kinks, say, or the Yardbirds, let alone the Rolling Stones.

Yet there was never a doubt. Three decades later, because of their longevity, the Stones may appear to have been their equals, but that is a trick of false perspective. In the beginning there was no contest. The Stones' most passionate early support came from minorities—rhythm and blues fans, London elitists, gays, nasty girls. The Beatles, by contrast, owned the masses. Their records sold more, their images fronted more magazines. Above all, the press at every level, from the tabloids to *The Times*, instinctively adored them.

What was the nature of their magic? Put in the crudest terms, they made people feel good. The same cheek and group confidence that so outraged the jazzmen in Ronnie Scott's was irresistible elsewhere. England in the early '60s was just beginning to emerge from 30 years of misery—the Depression, the War and the decade of aus-

January 17, 1964, at the George V hotel in Paris:
The boys find out "I Want to Hold Your Hand" is the No. 1 song in America.

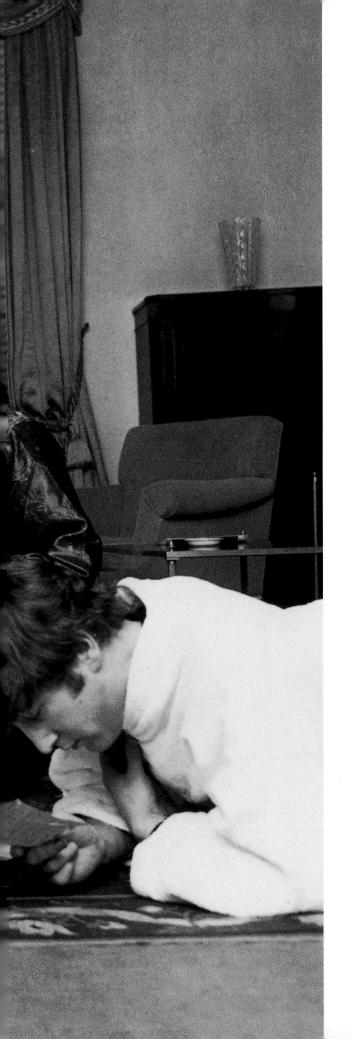

terity that had followed. For the first time in most people's memory, there was a little spare cash around. New clothes, new luxuries and vanities, a whole new sense of style. The country had a fresh spirit. And the Beatles were its embodiment.

Their music, at first, seemed almost an afterthought. Numbers like "Twist and Shout" and "I Saw Her Standing There" showed attack, a raw energy, but not much scope. Their real power lay in their personalities. They seemed to possess a secret shared understanding, some kind of instinctive group strength that made outsiders yearn to be included, middle-aged journalists as fiercely as besotted schoolgirls, even though they knew there was no way in. The Beatles' very exclusiveness was at the heart of their allure.

That quality of self-containment was, I think, crucial to their invasion of America. Watch the newsreels of them deplaning at Kennedy, or of their appearance on *The Ed Sullivan Show,* and they look like the four limbs of a single anatomy. Separate them, and they perish. Only as a group do they have a real life.

Impossible at that time to think of them ever breaking up. Their whole power was in their unity. The vague sense of the robotic that hung around them—identical outfits and hairstyles, interchangeable one-liners, their toneless Liverpool drone—lent them a crucial strangeness. They seemed almost like time-travelers, come from another dimension, as if they were on a private mission, sworn to show the rest of us what we'd been missing. *Look and listen,* they seemed to say. *Life is not so hard, after all. Forget the deprivation, the ugliness, the hurt. Come with us, and there will be no pain.*

The message meshed perfectly with the moment. If England was in slow and grudging recovery from its postwar austerities, America was in headlong riot. President Kennedy's assassination, a few months before the Beatles' arrival in the U.S., had been a shattering blow. But now these English invaders, in their youth and freshness, offered renewed hope.

If the Beatles helped energize America, however, America had an equal effect on them. Removed from their working-class roots, exposed to alien values and perspectives, they were forced to learn a whole other language. And this profoundly changed their music. As first Lennon and McCartney, and then George Harrison, began to develop and deepen as songwriters, the band's focus

Still in their pajamas at three p.m., they tackle a pile of mail.
No kidding: Ringo gets the most.

diffused. Less and less, from the mid-'60s on, were the Beatles defined by their physical presence. They were driven by words now. Soon those words became philosophies.

As their lyrics became more important, their reliance on hype and image began, if not to fade away, at least to evolve. Out went Brian Epstein's uniforms, and in came their own—the robes and beads, the trappings of Eastern mysticism, the facial hair. They didn't recognize these as uniforms, of course; to the Beatles themselves, they were a declaration of independence. With each successive album—*Help!, Rubber Soul, Revolver*—the Beatles became less of a product, more an interaction of four individuals. Their sense of group identity was fading.

In a way, by starting to spell out their beliefs, they stripped themselves of their deepest power. Their subliminal message had always been dead simple; nothing much more fancy than *Everything is going to be all right.* But what was simple, therefore strong, when unspoken, became merely simplistic when turned into anthems like "Let It Be" or "All You Need Is Love," and the difference proved fatal. The moment they started to promise utopia out loud, they nailed themselves to a platform. If ever that platform rotted, the crash was bound to be cruel hard.

It's easy to see now that the gradual weakening merely echoed their time. As the '60s began to wind down, doubts encroached. There was an increasing stridency to hippie polemic, a desperate refusal to face realities. The Beatles might sing "All You Need Is Love." But who, undrugged and unblinkered, could seriously believe them? When a growing list of disasters—Charles Manson, the assassination of Martin Luther King, the unending miseries in Vietnam—gave utopia the lie?

Only by devout use of LSD could the vision of Paradise Won be sustained. I remember a party in London, sometime in the summer of 1967, the long summer of *Sgt. Pepper.* By this time the Beatles had ceased to be a group, the property of screaming schoolgirls. They were now become artists, visionaries, mystical symbols. To the acid-riddled guests at the party, a cross section of King's Road glitterati—photographers, screenwriters, models, drug dealers and upper-class hippies—they were simply the ultimate heroes.

On this night, *Sgt. Pepper* played over and over; no other music existed. The general view was that this was the greatest record ever made, indeed the greatest work of art in any form, and when I dared to disagree, I was looked upon as a vile traducer. No good to say that it was a nice album, or that I liked some of the tunes; anything short of blind worship was tantamount to treason.

The fanaticism was more than a matter of music alone. To these people, the Beatles had done nothing less than reinvent the world. Future generations would look back on *Sgt. Pepper* as the dawning of a new cosmos. No more hatred and no more loss, no more pain, only love unconfined, and all of it due to the Fab Four.

I feel fine: caught in the act of composing a hit song
in those heady days of 1964.

It was an impossible burden for any beings to bear. Small wonder that the Beatles cracked and splintered beneath the strain; small wonder, either, that their idolaters could not forgive them for that. Two or three years later, when the euphoria of Woodstock and Monterey had foundered, and *Sgt. Pepper* was just another record, I came across some of the survivors from the King's Road party again, and their loathing of their lost gods was almost as intense as their former adoration.

It was as if they felt they'd been deliberately cheated, sucked in and then betrayed out of spite. I recall one bereft hairdresser breaking down in tears, for all the world like a bride left at the altar. "How could they?" he kept crying.

"How could they what?" I felt like asking, but there was really no need. I already knew what he meant: *How could they turn out human? Why hadn't they stayed gods?*

Was it all a con job, then? A modern variation of "The Emperor's New Clothes"? If one considers the Beatles simply as a social and political force, it is certainly tempting to think so. For all the devotion they roused at the time, the long-term fruits of their sermonizing seem scant indeed. A few grizzled survivors in California and upstate New York may still flash peace signs and mumble toothlessly of bliss. For the rest of the planet, it's as if Flower Power had never been.

The music itself, though, is not so easily dismissed. Some of it has dated. The early rockers sound clumsy today, and many of Paul McCartney's ballads—"Michelle," "Yesterday," even "Eleanor Rigby"—seem hopelessly mushy. Yet the best of their work, especially when John Lennon dominates, is as riveting as ever. Play "Strawberry Fields Forever," say, or "I Am The Walrus," churning and half-crazed and unforgettable. Or "Ticket to Ride" or "Help!"—there is a vitality there, a freshness of invention and a melodic richness, that the passage of years cannot touch.

Of late, there's been a resurgence in Beatlemania, both among musicians and a new generation of listeners. Anyone who tunes in to Top 40 radio in the '90s can hear echoes of Lennon/McCartney at every turn. Billy Joel, George Michael and Elton John, R.E.M. and Michael Jackson, Nirvana, Hootie and the Blowfish, the artist formerly known as Prince—the list of borrowers is endless. Not all the debts have been happy ones, but that is not the point. Strictly in terms of their musical influence, the Beatles remain immense.

And yet, in spite of that, their deepest impact goes beyond music. Now as in the beginning, their primary power lies in their own personae. Four rude boys, out of nowhere, off to conquer worlds. They gave off a sense of certainty, a nerveless ease, that grows more seductive with each passing year. In this era of grunge, racked by suicides and needles, the Beatles' cool insouciance seems like something from a golden age. For them, there were no bounds that couldn't be broken, no visions that couldn't come true. That may have been their folly. It was also their glory.

February 7, 1964, New York City's Kennedy Airport:
The Beatles have landed.

CHAPTER ONE

Liverpool was a tough place in the early 1940s—

a cold, gray port city where sailors and longshoremen worked hard, drank well, boasted loudly and,

when they had differences, fought them out in the streets. The city needed all its toughness, for Hitler

was intent on bombing it to smithereens. It was neither a pretty place to grow up nor a particular-

ly nurturing one. But Liverpool had a saving grace: Liverpudlians. Their dry wit and their flat Scouse

accents would one day become famous as Beatlespeak, and it's worth remembering that no pro-

ducer or imagemaker cooked it up. With little to look forward to except hard work, the people of

Liverpool somehow managed to retain their spunk—much like working people in the American

South, where rock and roll took root. No one could have predicted that this gritty, wounded city

would give birth to the world's greatest band. Then again, it makes perfect sense.

by Charles Hirshberg

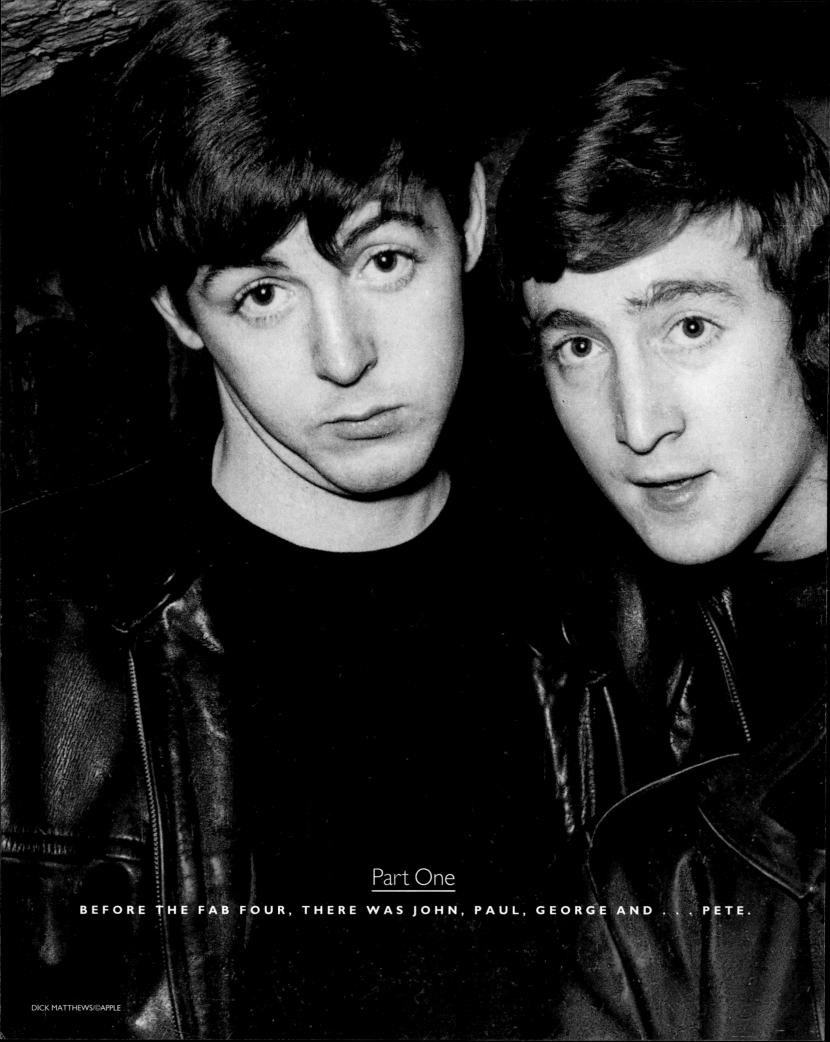

Part One

BEFORE THE FAB FOUR, THERE WAS JOHN, PAUL, GEORGE AND . . . PETE.

1940

Ringo arrives on July 7, 1940, the world's first Beatle baby. His given name is Richard Starkey. His father, a baker also named Richard Starkey, has a tough time being the world's first Beatle daddy. Before little Richie is four, big Richie leaves his wife, Elsie, and their delicate, big-eyed only child (right, in 1948). The lad proves both sickly and accident-prone. At six he suffers a ruptured appendix and spends two months in a coma. Then, while offering a toy bus to the boy in the next hospital bed, he tumbles headfirst to the floor, suffering a concussion. **His boyhood nickname is not "Ringo" but "Lazarus,"** and chronic pleurisy lands him in the hospital from 1953 to 1955. His lack of schooling gains him an undeserved reputation for stupidity—so much so, he later says, that when he joins his first band at age 16, he is assigned to drums because everyone assumes it is "the only thing I could do."

John Winston Lennon enters with a bang—a lot of bangs—on October 9, 1940, a night when Liverpool suffers a most horrific Nazi air raid. John's father, Alfred "Freddie" Lennon, a sailor, sees little of his son until 1946 (about the time of the photos at right). That year he takes the lad on holiday to Blackpool and decides to emigrate to New Zealand with him. Luckily, John is rescued by his mum, Julia. But she will always be more a friend than a parent, and John is raised almost entirely by his crusty but lovable aunt Mary "Mimi" Smith and her soft-touch husband, George. Ambition isn't John's strong suit—he hopes to run off to sea one day and become a ship's steward—until May 1956, **when he hears Elvis Presley sing "Heartbreak Hotel."** "From then on, I never got a minute's peace," Aunt Mimi later says. "It was Elvis Presley, Elvis Presley, Elvis Presley. In the end, I said, 'Elvis Presley's all very well, John, but I don't want him for breakfast, dinner *and* tea.'"

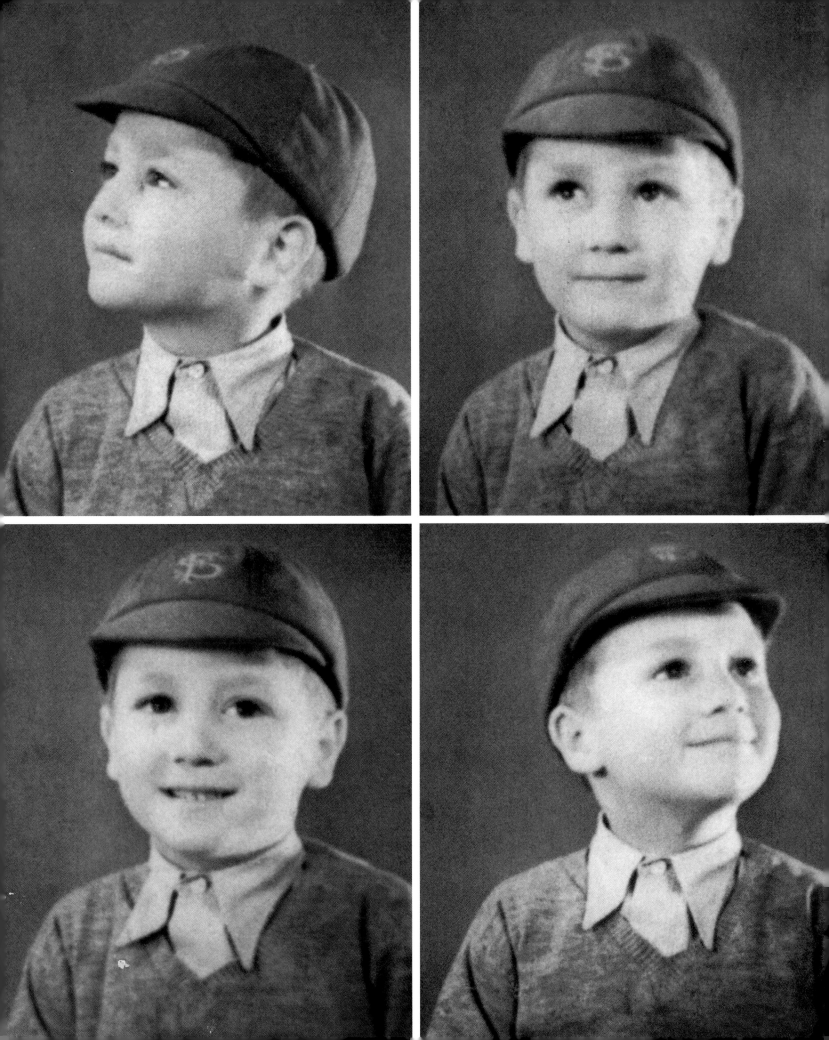

1942

Paul McCartney is born in Liverpool on June 18, 1942, to a musical heritage. His father, James, was once leader of Jim Mac's Jazz Band and sometimes composes his own songs (such as "Walking in the Park With Eloise," which Paul & Wings will record in 1974 under the pseudonym "The Country Hams"). James, whose day jobs include cleaning inspector and cotton salesman, plays music hall tunes in the evenings on the family piano, doubtless inspiring such classics as "When I'm Sixty-Four" and "Lovely Rita." **Paul's childhood is a middle-class idyll** compared with those of John and Ringo. (The photo below shows him at the age of seven, with his mother, Mary, and younger brother Michael.) But the idyll ends in 1956, when Mary, a nurse loved for her compassion and mildness, dies of breast cancer.

George Harrison is born in Liverpool on February 25, 1943, to music-loving bus driver Harold Hargreaves Harrison and his music-loving wife, Louise, a couple known at the Liverpool Corporation Centre for Conductors and Drivers as top-notch ballroom dancers. George loves music as soon as he discovers it: "I remember as a baby **standing on a leather stool, singing 'One Meat Ball.'**" He is a phenomenally bad student, finding school at best "a pain in the neck" and, at bottom, "the worst time in my life." He's a lucky flunk-out, though, "fortunate enough to feel there's an alternative." That alternative commences when Louise spends approximately $8 to buy him his first guitar at the age of 13, about the time of this portrait.

1 9 4 3

1957

7/6 St. Peter's Church in Liverpool seems an unlikely setting for one of the signal events in pop music history, but the Lord of Rock works in mysterious ways. It is here, on this day, that **John Lennon, 16, meets Paul McCartney, 15.** The Quarry Men, John's skiffle band (skiffle's a British version of jug band music), had been up and stumbling since March. A Saturday afternoon garden fete at St. Peter's (miraculously captured in the top photo) is the latest in an irregular series of gigs. Bassist Ivan Vaughan has invited his pal Paul to the show. During a break, Paul wows John with "Be-Bop-A-Lula." Even more impressive is his ability to tune a guitar, something John has been paying a neighbor to do. Two weeks later, Paul's a Quarry Man. His looks, along with new costumes (bottom), make the band appear more fetching, but their sound remains ragged. Over the next year and a half, they play an odd assortment of engagements, from the Morgue Skiffle Cellar to the Stanley Abattoir Social Club.

HULTON DEUTSCH

"

We arrived one Saturday afternoon at this guy's house on the outskirts of Liverpool and went into a back room where there were some very large machines on a table. There was a piano in the room, and we managed to squeeze ourselves in. We ran through two numbers. One was 'That'll Be the Day,' the old Buddy Holly number. The B side was 'In Spite Of All the Danger,' an original Paul wrote. We left that recording studio with one cut acetate disk, and that's the only one that ever existed. A month after, we'd all lost interest in it because the things coming over from America were so much better—Elvis, Jerry Lee Lewis, Little Richard, Chuck Berry. So it was forgotten.

JOHN "DUFF" LOWE *played piano for the Quarry Men in 1958 when the group recorded Paul McCartney's first original song, only recently released on The Beatles Anthology. In 1992 he revived the Quarry Men.*

"

1959

11/15 Although the Quarry Men inspire little admiration in the masses, they're revered by a youthful George (far right, with a later incarnation of the band), who gloms on to Paul on the bus to school and won't let go. Never formally inducted into the band, he is tolerated like a kid brother. In October they enter a competition to appear on *TV Star Search*. **They lose to a group led by a 4½-foot midget** but qualify for the regional finals in Manchester on this date. There, they find that the last bus leaves before curtain call and go home dejected. A row on the way results in the resignation of drummer Colin Hanton.

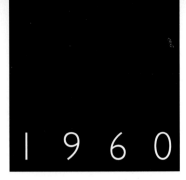

1960

5/10 "A right load of lay-abouts." That's what coffee-bar owner Allan Williams thinks of John Lennon and his art school chum, Stuart Sutcliffe. Sutcliffe, a talented painter, sells one of his works for $180, buys a bass, joins John's band and suggests a new name: Beatles. Soon after, **the lads do a great job repainting the ladies' loo** in Williams's café, and his opinion of them begins to change. When Williams discovers rock and roll—"I could smell money, lots of it"—he determines to manage the group and arranges an audition on this date with pop impresario Larry Parnes.

5/20 Parnes sends the Silver Beatles—as Williams has renamed them—to Scotland as back-up band for singer Johnny Gentle. Three days into the tour, Gentle crashes the van and **drummer Tommy Moore is hit flush in the mouth by a flying guitar;** his bandmates drag him from the hospital to play a gig. The Silver Beatles split $50 in weekly wages, insufficient to sustain life. They take to cadging meals and running out on hotel bills.

8/6 After their return from Scotland, the Silver Beatles learn from Williams of an opportunity in Germany: **A strip club on the Reeperbahn in Hamburg's red-light district** is starting to book rock and roll acts. But Tommy Moore has quit as drummer, and the Silver Beatles can't go until one is found. Fortune smiles: On this night the lads visit the Casbah Coffee Club and there, drumming with a band called the Blackjacks, is a handsome 18-year-old named Randolph Peter Best (see page 21). He's given a perfunctory audition, and two weeks later they all sail for Germany.

8/17 The Beatles begin performing at Bruno Koschmider's Indra club on this, the night of their arrival in Hamburg. They play for seven weeks, despite tiny, hostile audiences, complaints from neighbors and subhuman living conditions in the Bambi Kino, a movie theater across the street. Finally, Koschmider orders them to his more popular Kaiserkeller, where design student Klaus Voormann catches their act. He loves them and returns with his girlfriend, Astrid Kirchherr. She's even more smitten, particularly with Stu (at center), to whom she becomes engaged. (Stu will leave the band to live blissfully with Astrid but will die of a brain hemorrhage in 1962.) **Astrid gives the Beatles a makeover**—leather clothes, *those* haircuts—and takes these classic portraits (also see pages 32-33). The Beatles heat up and land a lucrative offer from a rival club, the Top Ten. Koschmider is furious, and suddenly Paul and Pete are arrested for arson, and George is deported for being underage. The lads regroup in England and return triumphantly to the Top Ten the following April. In Hamburg they record their first single, backing fellow Brit Tony Sheridan on a rock treatment of "My Bonnie."

1 9 6 1

7/3 The Beatles return from Hamburg still raw but with a habit of exploding onstage and a talent for making audiences explode back. Nowhere do they combust more exuberantly—or more regularly—than at Liverpool's Cavern Club, a onetime produce warehouse on Mathew Street (right). When the boys are on the bill, customers queue up for the privilege of walking **down 18 stone steps into dank, sweaty darkness,** where emcee Bob Wooler greets them: "Hi, all you Cavern dwellers! Welcome to the best of cellars!"

1 9 6 1

11/9 The ride to fame commences simply: Someone asks Brian Epstein, 27, manager of Liverpool's finest music store, if he stocks "My Bonnie." He doesn't and wonders why not. What is this band, this record, this Cavern, that the youth of Liverpool are chattering about? On this date, Epstein drops into the club ("a black deep grave," he will later call it) and sees them, much as they appear here: **"captivating, honest . . . and not very clean."** Less than a month later, despite a warning from his family solicitor—and one from Allan Williams, stiffed by the Beatles, who advises he not touch them "with a barge pole"—Epstein promises that for 25 percent of the proceeds, he'll land them better gigs and a record deal. "Right, then, Brian," says John. "Manage us."

DICK MATTHEWS/©APPLE

Part Two

WITH RINGO ABOARD AND BRIAN AT THE HELM, THE MOPTOPS TAKE ON THE WORLD.

1 9 6 2

9/11 From the moment Brian Epstein (opposite) signs the Beatles until the end of his short life, he will spend nearly every moment working in their behalf. His first task is to get them a record deal. Problem: Nobody wants them. Brian wangles an audition with Decca Records, but executive Dick Rowe says "guitar groups are on the way out." Finally, George Martin, head of EMI's Parlophone, best known for comedy records, agrees to hear the band. Martin decides to proceed with a recording session but has one unpleasant proviso. Pete Best—whom Martin describes bluntly as "not good"—will not play. On August 16 it's Brian's unsavory task to **tell Pete he's out.** Liverpool fans are mad as hell; some vandalize Brian's car. Best's replacement is a friend from Hamburg times: Ringo Starr, of Rory Storm and the Hurricanes, who had filled in on "My Bonnie." On this day, with both Starr and session drummer Andy White on percussion, the band cuts "Love Me Do" (John and Paul in the studio, right). The song hits U.K. charts at No. 49; rumor has it Brian bought some 10,000 copies.

1 9 6 3

2/11 Martin puts the final touches to "Please Please Me," saying, "Gentlemen, you've just made **your first number one.**" He's right, and decides to cut an album "straightaway." At 10 a.m. this day, the Beatles enter EMI's studio; by 10:45 p.m., they've recorded 10 songs. The LP will spend 30 weeks atop the British charts.

10/13 Public appearances are now so frequent a Beatle hardly has time for primping (at left, backstage before a concert). In March the band is slated to tour with American star Tommy Roe. But it's obvious from opening-night screams that the billing is topsy-turvy, and the appearance schedule is reversed. In May they try opening for Roy Orbison, whom they idolize. Same result, same remedy. That summer, *Pop Goes the Beatles* debuts on BBC radio and exposes all Britain to their sound and their wacky brand of humor. (Often the butt of their jokes is emcee Lee Peters, whom they refer to off-mike as Pee Liters.) But it is on this autumn night that the lid comes off. The lads appear on *Val Parnell's Sunday Night at the London Palladium,* a TV show with 15 million viewers. The live audience becomes so excited and unruly that at one point John shouts, "Shut up!" **Fleet Street coins a new term** for what's happening: Beatlemania.

ILFORD   H P 3

1   1A   2   2A   3   3A

ILFORD   H P 3

7   7A   8   8A   9   9A

ILFORD   H P 3

19   19A   20   20A   21   21A

ILFORD   H P 3   HYPERSENSITIVE

26   26A   27   27A   28   28A

HYPERSENSITIVE   PANCHROMATIC

4   4A   5   5A   6   6A

HYPERSENSITIVE   PANCHROMATIC

10   10A   11   11A   12   12A

HYPERSENSITIVE   PANCHROMATIC

22   22A   23   23A   25   25A

PANCHROMATIC

29   29A   30   30A   31   31A

1 9 6 3

10/31 Returning to London's Heathrow Airport after a triumphant tour of Sweden—during which George was nearly dragged from the stage by hysterical Stockholmers—the band is met by **hundreds of screeching fans** and more than 100 reporters. As fate will have it, an American awaiting his flight observes the ruckus. He is Ed Sullivan, whose business is sniffing out the next big thing. He soon books the Beatles for his show.

11/4 Before tonight's Royal Command Performance, at the invitation of Queen Elizabeth, John horrifies Brian by threatening to ask the gilded audience to "rattle their f---in' jewelry." But onstage, he is all charm: "Would the people in the cheap seats clap your hands? And the rest of you, if you'll just rattle your jewelry." The gig—not to mention the gag—is a triumph. The Beatles have been stamped with **the Royal Seal of Approval,** making criticism of the naughty rock and rollers all but impossible.

11/16 So much for Britain, where George (right) and his mates have become **prisoners of their celebrity.** Can they also conquer America, rock's cradle, where English emulators have never thrived? The media consensus is no. CBS News correspondent Alexander Kendrick, reporting from this evening's concert in Bournemouth, explains to stateside viewers that the Beatles "symbolize the 20th century nonhero, as they make nonmusic." *The New York Times* predicts "Beatlemania will [not] be successfully exported." But already a bootleg version of "I Want to Hold Your Hand" is finding its way to a Washington, D.C., radio station, and the capital's kids are pricking up their ears.

12/13 It has been less than two years since Brian Epstein (second from right) defiantly promised a group of scornful record company officials that one day his Beatles would be **"bigger than Elvis."** But if the British recording industry has been slow to listen, the Americans have been positively deaf. Even Capitol Records—like Parlophone, owned by EMI—has stubbornly declined to distribute Beatle records in the States. "We don't think the Beatles will do anything in this market," the company's president has said. Consequently, their first three singles are released on the tiny Vee Jay and Swan labels, with predictably modest sales. But on this date, Capitol executives finally admit their mistake and sign a distribution agreement. Two weeks later they release "I Want to Hold Your Hand."

1 9 6 4

2/7 "I Want to Hold Your Hand" rockets to No. 1 on the U.S. charts, and, on this day, Pan Am Flight 101 rockets across the Atlantic bearing four rather insecure moptops. "They've got everything over there," says George. "What do they want *us* for?" At Kennedy Airport, 3,000 hysterical Beatlemaniacs greet them. When the lads first glimpse the crowd, they figure the President must be landing. Two days later, **a record 73 million people watch them** on *The Ed Sullivan Show* (below), including a lucky few in the studio audience (right). The first name of each Beatle is superimposed on the screen. John's caption has a P.S.: "Sorry, Girls, He's Married."

I remember hearing 'I Want to Hold Your Hand,' and all of a sudden, for the first time in my life, I started dancing. It seemed that the years of wartime repression were really over, or something was over, and the new era had begun. People were returning back into their bodies unafraid and were celebrating their physical existence—the dance, which is an old, human ritual. Everybody was moved to dance.

ALLEN GINSBERG *is the author of the Beat Generation anthem "Howl."*

HARRY BENSON

HENRY GROSSMAN

1 9 6 4

2/11 Their first U.S. concert is in the nation's capital on this day, and even as John and his mates are riding the train down from New York (left), excitement is building. Though *The Washington Post* has described the Beatles as "asexual and homely," more than 7,000 fans will jam the Coliseum (next page) to decide for themselves. At a British Embassy reception, as the group obligingly signs autographs, one upper-class twit asks, "Can they actually *write*?" Another **walks up to Ringo and cuts off a piece of his hair.** Back in London, the foreign secretary is called upon to explain why the Beatles are being treated in such an undignified manner, but in the Colonies everyone's having a good laugh. When Prime Minister Sir Alec Douglas-Home arrives at the White House the next morning for a meeting with President Johnson, LBJ is all smiles. "I like your advance guard," he says. "But don't you think they need haircuts?"

1 9 6 4

GLOBE PHOTOS

2/22 Their visit lasts only two weeks, but that's enough for America to fall **head over heels in love with the Fab Four.** They're so *cute,* they just have to be kissed (even Ringo, above in Miami Beach). The squarest of square Yanks are disarmed by their sense of humor. "Have you got a leading lady for your movie?" George is asked. "We're trying to get the queen," he replies. "She sells." Another reporter asks Paul, "What do you think of the campaign in Detroit to stamp out the Beatles?" He answers: "We've got a campaign of our own—to stamp out Detroit!" John is asked, "Was your family in show business?" to which he responds, "Well, me dad used to say me mother was a great performer." Outside New York City's Plaza Hotel, where the Beatles camp for four days, hundreds of teenage girls hold a nonstop vigil, chanting "She Loves You." The boys return home on this date, but not before Ed Sullivan pays tribute: "These youngsters from Liverpool, England, and their conduct over here, not only as fine professional singers but as a group of fine youngsters, will leave an imprint on everyone who's met them."

It was a Thursday, and we were out doing stuff. My mom told us we weren't going to school the next day. Then she told us what was going on and said we couldn't tell anybody. You want to act cool, like you're not fazed, but inside it's pretty much, 'Wow, the Beatles are in my house!' . . . They were just real playful. They were like kids.

LINDA POLLAK-SULLIVAN, *now a freelance writer, was 15 when LIFE arranged for the Beatles to visit her house in Miami (right).*

BOB GOMEL

MOVIE STILL ARCHIVES

7/10 Some 200,000 Liverpudlians—more than a quarter of the city—line the streets to welcome their hometown heroes for the premiere of *A Hard Day's Night.* "Fresh and engaging," says *Time.* "Fresh and lively," counters *Newsweek.* Historian Arthur Schlesinger Jr. calls it **"the astonishment of the month"**—meaning it's actually *good!* Can we look forward to any more Beatle movies? "Well, there'll be many more," John replies. "But I don't know whether you can look forward to them."

8/18 The Ever-Fabber Four arrive in San Francisco for a monster tour of America: 26 concerts in 34 days. Waiting for them is Charles O. Finley, owner of the Kansas City A's baseball team. He has personally promised the state of Missouri a Beatles concert. He offers Brian $50,000. Brian says no. A week later, Finley offers a check for $100,000. Epstein says no. Finley writes a $150,000 check. Brian agrees to "ask the boys," who are playing cards in the next room. "Whatever you want," John says, barely looking up from his hand. It's another record: **$4,838 a minute for a live show.**

3/2 Ten days after their return from America, the Beatles begin shooting *A Hard Day's Night*—mostly scenes of **Fabs on the run** from their fans. Sometimes, director Richard Lester tells his cameraman to "keep turning" as they flee real-life Beatlemaniacs on the set (above).

ROBERT FREEMAN/©APPLE

9/11 Florida's Gator Bowl is the most memorable stop on their second American tour, for they arrive to find that Hurricane Dora has preceded them. So has President Johnson, who has declared Jacksonville a disaster area. On top of that, the show had almost been canceled days earlier—for reasons entirely unrelated to the tempest. Revolted by the racial tension they'd seen throughout America, the band had insisted it would play the Dixie venue only with assurances that the audience would not be segregated. In the end, the Fabs take the stage with **40-mile-an-hour winds whipping through their moptops.** Ringo's drums have to be nailed to the stage to keep them from blowing away.

CHARLES TRAINOR

Part Three

AFTER THREE YEARS OF BEATLEMANIA, THE BOYS DECIDE TO HIDE THEMSELVES AWAY.

1 9 6 5

6/11 In one two-week swing the band plays 15 shows in France, Italy and Spain. It seems the cheeky kids are **their country's best ambassadors.** Today that fact is sanctioned with an announcement: The Beatles are to join the Most Excellent Order of the British Empire. Says John: "I thought you had to drive tanks and win wars to get the MBE."

7/29 Director Richard Lester's challenge: to make a second Beatles film as appealing as *A Hard Day's Night* without simply copying it. In *Help!*, he gives each Beatle more of an individual identity, based loosely on real life. George is depicted as a romantic miser; Ringo as lovable and self-effacing; John as witty and sardonic, and Paul as the redoubtable ladies' man (hence, this cheesecake scene from the film). During much of the shooting—which takes place in the Bahamas and Austria, as well as Britain—**Paul drives Lester crazy** by spending his breaks at a piano, plunking a tune he's working on. "If I hear that once more," Lester finally says, "I'll have that bloody piano taken away. What's it called, anyway?" "'Scrambled Egg,'" Paul replies. The finished film premieres on this date to lukewarm reviews, but Paul will soon send Lester a record with a note: "I hope you like 'Scrambled Egg.'" Lester recognizes the hated melody immediately—even though Paul has changed its title from "Scrambled Egg" to "Yesterday."

1 9 6 5

8/15 A concert at New York City's Shea Stadium **breaks records for rock-show attendance** (55,600), gross ($304,000) and fee ($160,000 to the band). Two weeks later, as if to crown the achievement, the Fab Four enjoy an audience with Elvis himself at his Hollywood digs. So what now? Is it possible to go any higher? The answer comes in December, when the Beatles release *Rubber Soul*. The album takes pop music to a new level, especially with "Norwegian Wood." It features a haunting melody, a sitar and obscure modernist lyrics Elvis could never have imagined.

10/26 Despite a bit of controversy—a Canadian returns his MBE rather than sink to "the same level as vulgar nincompoops"—surging **crowds buck the bobbies at Buckingham** (right) as the Beatles arrive on this day to receive their medals. Says Paul: "We've played Frisco's Cow Palace but never one like this. It's a keen pad." And Her Majesty—a pretty nice girl? "She was like a mum to us."

HULTON DEUTSCH

1966

6/24 For four years, the Beatles have gone from triumph to triumph—every record a hit, every concert a rave—but now they begin a two-week tour of Europe and Asia, during which they will not only stumble but be kicked as well. It begins with two concerts in Munich on this day. "Rehearsals," such as they are, take place in the dressing room (left) and prove insufficient: Paul repeatedly garbles the lyrics of "I'm Down," and George flubs the introduction of "Yesterday." In Asia, the following week, it only gets worse. First, hypercautious **Tokyo police confine them to their hotel** and manhandle their fans. Then, after missing an appointment with Imelda Marcos, they're jostled at the Manila airport by angry Filipinos. "We're going to have a couple of weeks to recuperate," George tells the English press when the band returns to London, "before we go and get beaten up by the Americans."

1966

8/11 It had all started in March, when John shared with a reporter his conviction that "Christianity will vanish"—bolstering his claim by arguing that the Beatles "are **more popular than Jesus** now." Many Americans, particularly in the Bible Belt, were incensed. Beatle records were banned by 22 radio stations, and a rash of "Beatle Burnings" followed—public incinerations of albums and merchandise (here a Fort Oglethorpe, Ga., bonfire). Horrified, Brian Epstein had considered canceling the group's American tour, despite being advised it might

cost a million dollars. "I'll pay it out of my own pocket," he'd said, quite sincerely. "If anything were to happen to any one of them, I'd never forgive myself." Instead, the Beatles creep back to America, and, on this day, John apologizes meekly (right): "I'm sorry I opened my mouth. The record-burning, that was a real shock. I couldn't go away knowing that I'd created another little pocket of hate in the world. Especially with something as uncomplicated as people listening to records, dancing and enjoying what the Beatles are."

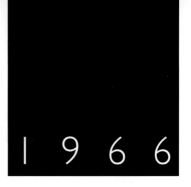

1966

8/29 The tour, which includes a return to Shea Stadium, damn near kills them. On August 19 they receive a death threat in Memphis, and when a firecracker goes off during the show, they think they're being shot at. The next day in Cincinnati a promoter who has failed to provide a stage canopy can't understand why the Beatles are unwilling to play electric guitars in a rainstorm. Thirty-five thousand hysterical fans are shown the door, and Paul is so agitated he becomes ill. On August 28, at Dodger Stadium, L.A. cops are seen beating teenage girls. **Dozens are trampled in the chaos.** At the final stop, on this day at Candlestick Park in San Francisco (pages 74-75), Brian tells a friend, "This is the last one ever." The Beatles know it too. John and Paul bring cameras to document a historic event—the last concert they will ever play.

SID BERNSTEIN, Presents

NO REFUNDS — NO EXCHANGES

SHEA STADIUM

ENTER GATE **C**

UPPER RESERVED $5.00

6 SEC.

V ROW

12 SEAT

TUE., AUG. 23, 1966-7:30 P.M.

When the Beatles were going to do Shea Stadium for the first time, Zal Yanovsky and me got into their drums at Manny's in New York. We wrote on them, 'Dear Beatles, Welcome to Amerikka—The Lovin' Spoonful,' and we taped some joints onto the drumheads. It was like the medium of exchange in the Sixties—you know, the peace pipe and showing that we were hip or whatever. When they later came to see us in England, George said, 'We appreciated very much your gift.'

JOE BUTLER
*is the lead
singer and
drummer for
The Lovin'
Spoonful.*

Part Four

THE BEATLES STRETCH THEIR MINDS AND THEIR MUSIC . . . UNTIL THE BAND SNAPS.

1 9 6 7

2/13 The Beatles' last bow is followed by **a period of sublime creativity.** It begins in November 1966, when John comes into the Abbey Road Studio with his acoustic guitar to play "Strawberry Fields Forever" for maestro producer George Martin (left, at the studio). Martin is so taken with the song that he tries two radically different approaches: a slow tempo with just the Beatles, a fast tempo with orchestra. John likes the beginning of the former, the end of the latter. So Martin speeds up one, slows down the other and splices them—creating one of the most innovative songs in pop music history. Shortly thereafter, Paul plays "Penny Lane" for Martin and says he wants the song to have a "special sound"—something akin to what he'd recently heard at a performance of Bach's *Brandenburg Concertos*. "There was a guy playing this fantastic high trumpet," Paul says. "Can we use it?" Martin hires David Mason of the London Symphony Orchestra, who contributes a spectacular solo on the piccolo trumpet, unlike anything heard before in rock music. The single featuring these two remarkable songs is released on this date. Martin will later call it "the best record we ever made."

They would experiment with sounding different, asking, 'Could we try something?' One day, making *Revolver*, John said how much he loved the sound when you weren't quite tuned in on a radio station, and it was sort of coming and going. [We] figured out a way of re-creating it—by splitting a signal and controlling the timing of the second signal so you hear a pitch change.

KEN SCOTT, *one of George Martin's engineers at Abbey Road, went on to work with David Bowie and Duran Duran.*

1 9 6 7

6/1 As the Beatles begin to assemble songs for their new album, **they discover inspiration everywhere**—in the innocent simplicity of childhood, the psychedelic phantasmagoria of LSD, and everything in between. "Mr. Kite" derives from an 1843 circus flyer; "Fixing a Hole" is born on Paul's roof; "Lucy in the Sky" is the sound track to a painting by John's four-year-old son, Julian. They experiment with a host of instruments, from an Indian swordmandel ("Within You Without You") to a bass harmonica ("Mr. Kite") to comb and paper ("Lovely Rita"). After taping the song "Sgt. Pepper," Paul hits on the idea of making a theme album, "as though Sgt. Pepper was making the recording." It is also his idea to sprinkle the album with sound effects, from a bizarre montage of Victorian steam organs to a rooster, whose crowing dissolves into the strains of a guitar. The photo session for the album's cover (left, an unused version) is the most elaborate ever, requiring legal releases from dozens of celebrities pictured in the backdrop—from Sonny Liston to William Burroughs to Shirley Temple Black. Finally, on this date, *Sgt. Pepper's Lonely Hearts Club Band* is released in the U.K. No less a connoisseur than Leonard Bernstein finds in it a power to "sustain me, rejuvenate me, inflame my senses and sensibilities."

I was walking with Paul McCartney on Primrose Hill one lovely spring day, and he was with Martha, his big English sheepdog. And we're walking around, and he was looking at the weather, and he said to me, 'It's getting better.' We walked a bit farther, and he said, 'It really is getting better. You've got to admit it's getting better.' And he started singing those two phrases and laughing. By the time we walked back to Paul's house, he'd worked up those few bars of the song.

HUNTER DAVIES, *author of the official Beatles biography, spent 18 months with the group in the era that included* Sgt. Pepper.

1 9 6 7

8/25 The lesson of *Sgt. Pepper* is simple, says Paul: "There aren't as many barriers as we'd thought." There seem to be none that can't be surmounted by Beatle music, Beatle drugs or, now, Transcendental Beatle Meditation. On this day, **the Fabs follow guru Maharishi Mahesh Yogi** to a weekend seminar in Wales (below). They are trailed by a crew of snickering reporters as they unwittingly set sail on a sea of disasters.

HENRY GROSSMAN

8/27 "Oh, Christ, no!" screams Paul into the phone, shattering their transcendental retreat. **Brian Epstein has been found dead** in his London apartment from an overdose of sleeping pills. Suicide is suspected. Brian—tortured by blackmailers' threats to reveal his homosexuality and terrified that his beloved Beatles might desert him—had already attempted it twice. But a coroner's report says his death was probably accidental. The Beatles will never fully recover. "After Brian died," John later says, "we collapsed. We broke up then. That was the disintegration."

© BBC

9/11 Paul gets the idea when he hears about Ken Kesey driving around the U.S. in that psychedelic bus full of Merry Pranksters. The Beatles should try that, Paul decides, and preserve the merry pranks on film! And so, on this day, **with a bizarre cast of dancers, midgets and strippers in tow,** they embark on a Magical Mystery Tour of England. But with no Brian to look after details, they meet with every conceivable snafu—even the Magical Mystery signs fall off the bus. When the finished product airs at Christmas (above, a scene from the movie), critics hammer it: "nonsense," "rubbish," "a bore." Paul rebuts: "Aren't we entitled to a flop? Was the film really so bad compared with the rest of the Christmas TV? You could hardly call the queen's speech a gasser."

1/22 The Beatles suddenly discover that **more than $4 million will be taken in taxes** unless it is used for business purposes. So, on this day, Apple Corps opens its Wigmore Street offices. ("It's a pun," explains Paul. "Apple *core.* See?") The company will sponsor such dubious ventures as Apple Electronics, run by one "Magic Alex" Mardas, whose wacky ideas include surrounding Ringo's drumstand with an electronic "wall of silence" made of ultrahigh-frequency beams. There will also be a pair of swiftly failing Apple boutiques and a never realized set of plans for Apple School, to serve "children ages two to forty." Only Apple Records, which releases albums by James Taylor and the Modern Jazz Quartet in addition to Beatles discs, will have any success.

7/17 Driven by contractual obligation, the Beatles unenthusiastically authorize production of a full-length cartoon (left). They contribute four songs to the project but little else—not even their speaking voices. On this night they attend the London premiere of *Yellow Submarine* . . . and get **a delightful surprise!** It's a gem, an instant animated classic.

8/22 What happened to the four happy moptops? Sessions for the "White Album" burn with friction until, amazingly, **the unflappable Ringo snaps** and, on this day, quits. It brings the others together: Each adds percussion to "Back in the U.S.S.R.," and when Ringo decides to return, he finds his drum kit bedecked with flowers.

1969

3/20 Only eight days after Paul shocks legions of love-struck fans by marrying American photographer Linda Eastman, John upstages him by marrying Japanese artist Yoko Ono. (She had introduced herself at a London gallery in 1966, handing him a card emblazoned with the word "Breathe.") Though publicly inseparable since the previous spring—around the time John's now-ex, Cynthia, discovered them together in her house—**the couple John calls "johnandyoko"** have, until today, seemed much too bohemian for marriage. Already famous for their "events"—avant-garde photo-ops like releasing 365 helium balloons over London or appearing onstage at the Royal Albert Hall in a white bag—they now embark upon a weeklong bed-in at the Amsterdam Hilton (right). Fifty salivating reporters arrive, apparently hoping to find the newlyweds in the act of copulation. Instead, notes one, the honeymooners do "nothing at all except clutch a tulip each." John explains that the bed-in is a "protest against all the suffering and violence in the world." Mischievously, he adds: "I hope it's not a letdown."

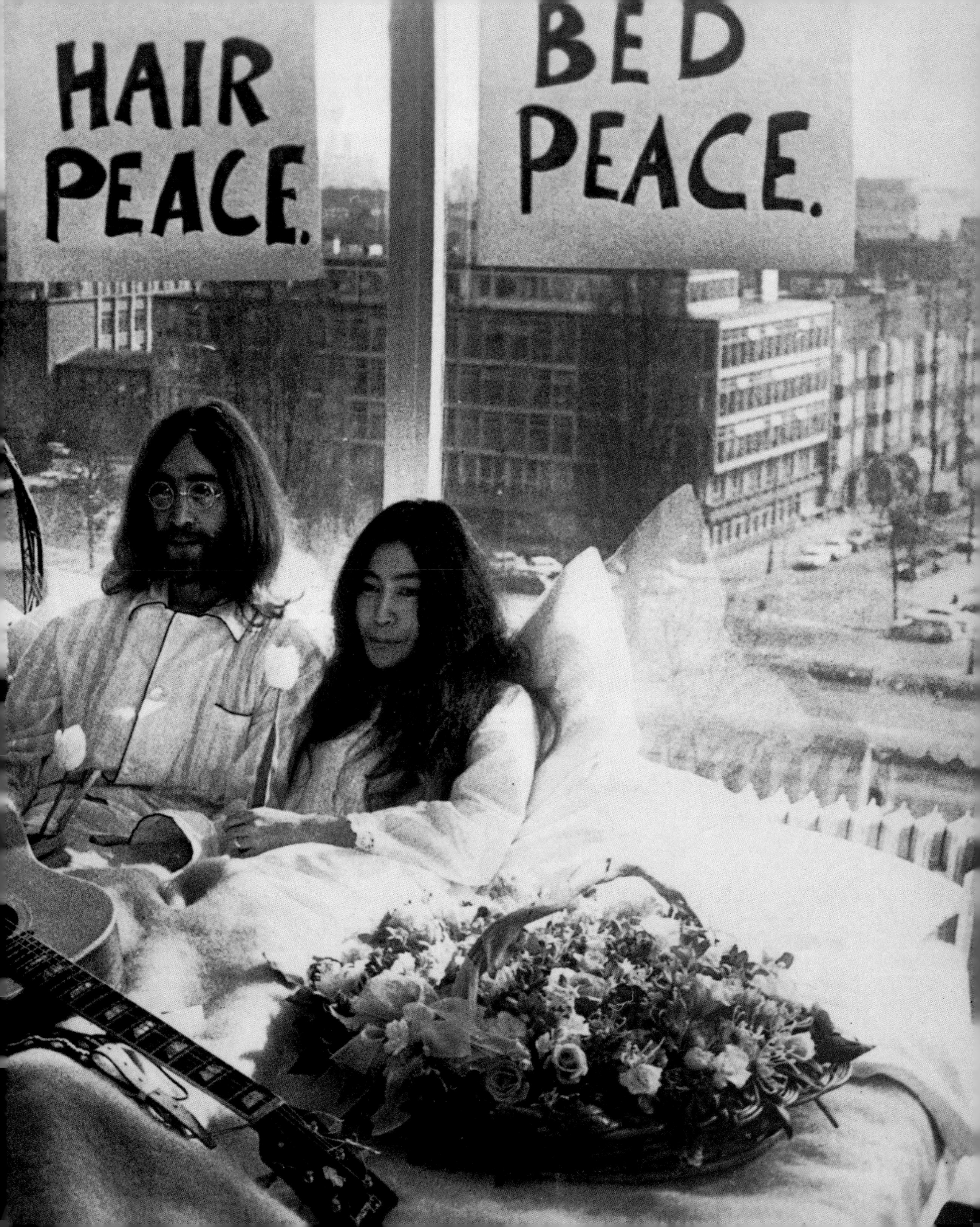
HAIR
PEACE.
BED
PEACE.

1 9 6 9

5/28 The band is fragmenting. Hoping to save the Beatles, Paul suggests their next album be bolstered by a concert. But nothing mundane: Perhaps they should play in an abandoned flour mill by the Thames, or aboard ship,

or in a Roman amphitheater in North Africa. Producer Dennis O'Dell arranges to film whatever happens in the studio (above)—but not much does. The closest thing to a concert is **a jam session on Apple's roof** (opposite). Finished on this date, the *Let It Be* album is deemed unworthy of release. Eventually the tapes are turned over to Phil Spector, who adds lush orchestrations to such songs as "The Long and Winding Road," infuriating Paul. John hates the album too, but doesn't blame Spector: "He was given the s----iest load of badly recorded s---, and he made something out of it."

9/26 A ferocious power struggle has emerged (reflected in the Linda McCartney photo on pages 90-91, which she called *The Four Strangers*). John wants New York showbiz accountant Allen Klein to **untangle the Beatles' chaotic finances;** Paul wants to entrust the job to his brother-in-law, attorney John Eastman. Lennon wins, but there is now enough ill will to finish off 10 bands. It seems a shame to end on such a dismal note: What if the boys have one great album left in them? There's only one way to find out. Paul meekly approaches George Martin to see if he'll agree to make a record "the way we used to do it." Martin replies sternly: "If all of you are the way *you* used to be." Says Paul: "We promise." Thus begins the recording of *Abbey Road*, released on this date and destined to become the best-selling Beatles album of all time.

1970

4/10 The last group portraits of the Beatles are taken by photographer Monte Fresco at Tittenhurst Park, John's estate near Ascot. The subjects (right) give no indication that a breakup is imminent, but a few weeks later, John will lay his cards on the table: "I want a divorce," he tells Paul. Still, for the next half year the band remains alive but comatose, as if no one can quite bear to pull the plug. Now there are plenty of clues: John is appearing publicly with his Plastic Ono Band; Ringo is recording an album of pop standards; George is touring with Eric Clapton and blue-eyed soulsters Delaney and Bonnie; Paul is off at his retreat in St. John's Wood, recording *McCartney*. That album is released on this date, along with a bombshell—a press release that stuns a world of Beatle fans, to say nothing of the other three Beatles. Paul says that owing to "personal differences, business differences, musical differences, but most of all because I have a better time with my family," **he is quitting the band.** "Temporary or permanent? I don't know." Later he will admit: "I think the manner of doing it, I regret. I wish I'd been a little kinder."

"Big bastards, that's what the Beatles were," says John. "Don't ever call me ex-Beatle McCartney again," says Paul. "We're not friends." As years pass, the acrimony waxes and wanes. Then, in May 1979, something wonderful happens: At Eric Clapton's wedding (to the former Mrs. Harrison), George, Paul and Ringo just stand up and start to jam. "It didn't feel strange at all," marvels Paul. "It'll be great to do one like that again, with just the four of us." But John is settled in New York City with Yoko and since Sean's birth in 1975 has found contentment at home. "I've been baking bread," he says proudly. "I took a Polaroid of my first loaf! And taking care of the baby is such a tremendous responsibility." In late 1980 he reemerges with *Double Fantasy*. He is in a buoyant mood when he welcomes photographer Annie Leibovitz to his apartment in the elegant Dakota building to take these pictures. "I am going into an unknown future," he tells a radio interviewer on this same day. "And while there's life, there's hope." That hope flickers out minutes before 11 p.m. when a deranged fan waiting outside the Dakota **empties his revolver into John Lennon's chest.** It is over quickly. John stumbles inside, scattering cassette tapes of his last recordings on the floor. Words still fail to express the senselessness of it, but two epitaphs linger: "Give peace a chance," chanted by mourners outside the Dakota, and Sean's farewell, "Now Daddy is part of God. I guess when you die you become much more bigger because you're part of everything." And Paul? He still can't quite believe the four will never play again: "It's like those dreams you have. He's still alive. Then you wake up and . . . 'Oh.'"

12/8
1 9 8 0

THE U.S. ALBUMS
(Pictured on facing page)

Introducing the Beatles
July 22, 1963
Vee Jay

Meet the Beatles
January 20, 1964
Capitol

The Beatles' Second Album
April 10, 1964
Capitol

A Hard Day's Night
June 26, 1964
United Artists

Something New
July 20, 1964
Capitol

The Beatles' Story
November 23, 1964
Capitol

Beatles '65
December 15, 1964
Capitol

THE U.K. ALBUMS

Please Please Me
March 22, 1963
Parlophone

The Early Beatles
March 22, 1965
Capitol

With the Beatles
November 22, 1963
Parlophone

Beatles VI
June 14, 1965
Capitol

A Hard Day's Night
July 10, 1964
Parlophone

Help!
August 13, 1965
Capitol

Beatles for Sale
December 4, 1964
Parlophone

Rubber Soul
December 6, 1965
Capitol

Help!
August 6, 1965
Parlophone

"Yesterday". . . And Today
June 20, 1966
Capitol

Rubber Soul
December 3, 1965
Parlophone

Revolver
August 8, 1966
Capitol

Revolver
August 5, 1966
Parlophone

Sgt. Pepper's Lonely Hearts Club Band
June 2, 1967
Capitol

A Collection of Beatles Oldies
December 10, 1966
Parlophone

Magical Mystery Tour
November 27, 1967
Capitol

Sgt. Pepper's Lonely Hearts Club Band
June 1, 1967
Parlophone

The Beatles
November 25, 1968
Apple (Capitol)

The Beatles
November 22, 1968
Apple (Parlophone)

Yellow Submarine
January 13, 1969
Apple (Capitol)

Yellow Submarine
January 17, 1969
Apple (Parlophone)

Abbey Road
October 1, 1969
Apple (Capitol)

Abbey Road
September 26, 1969
Apple (Parlophone)

Hey Jude
February 26, 1970
Apple (Capitol)

Let It Be
May 8, 1970
Apple (Parlophone)

Let It Be
May 18, 1970
Apple (Capitol)

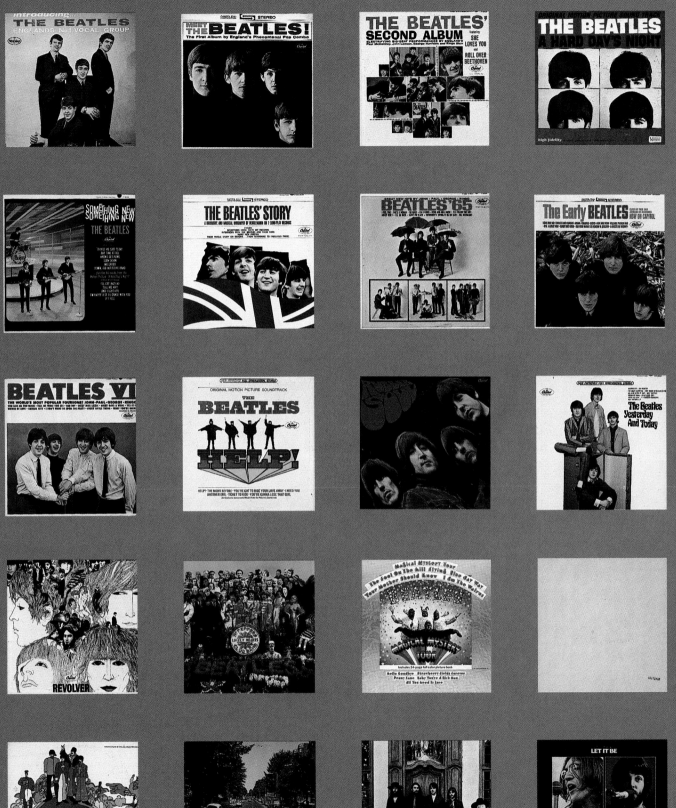

Today

They're a little like our children. It wasn't always

fun watching them grow up, and it can be downright painful watching them grow old. We

wince as they take off in some ill-considered direction, but know there's nothing we can do.

And then, when things work out better than we could ever have hoped, we're so happy for

them. The past quarter century has seen some brilliant flashes, some flashy failures, a few

flashbacks and the occasional blackout. From Wings to Wilburys; from *All You Need Is Cash*

to *Thomas the Tank Engine*; from the Top 10 to the 12-step program . . . the Beatles play on.

by Charles Hirshberg

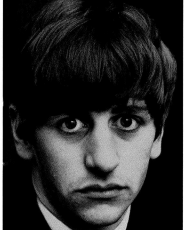

RINGO

What went wrong? His solo career had started so promisingly. The soulful "It Don't Come Easy" was a smash worthy of Paul or John. And the closest thing to a Beatles reunion had come when his three ex-mates each entered the studio (though never together) to play on his 1973 album, *Ringo*. All of this had been such a pleasant surprise. Then he went into free fall. "I just got caught up in that strange belief that if you're creative, you have to be brain-damaged," he later said. "But I wasn't creating anything. Unless you want to call *Thomas the Tank Engine and Friends* creating something." Actually, *Thomas,* a British children's TV show Ringo narrated in the 1980s, was pretty good, as was his subsequent turn as Mr. Conductor on the American kiddie show *Shining Time Station.* The problem, simply put, was that Mr. Conductor was a drunk. "I was just that personality person. I would be at all the parties with me bow tie on. If you were straight, I wouldn't have you in my house." His solo career went to pieces. He couldn't even find a record company to

Every awkward adolescent once had a hero in the Beatles' big-beaked drummer. Now he's a model of middle-aged survival.

The beat's been bumpy for Ringo since 1981, when he and Barbara were wed. But since reclaiming his sobriety, he's had plenty to twist and shout about.

release his recordings in the mid-1980s. About the only gig he could get was, ironically, as spokesman for a wine cooler, which gave him the dubious distinction of being the first Beatle to push a product. But in October 1988, Ringo faced facts and, along with his wife, actress Barbara Bach (they had met while filming the forgettable *Caveman*), entered a Tucson recovery clinic. Upon emerging, one of his first acts was to take legal action blocking any future release of recordings he had made in 1987 (with Bob Dylan's help)—recordings done, he said, in a "degenerative atmosphere." Then he assembled his All-Starr Band, with virtuosos such as Dr. John, Billy Preston and

Joe Walsh, and toured 30 cities. In the band's most recent incarnation, he shared drums with son Zak. "I'm not Pavarotti," says Ringo, now 55 and sober. "But I *do* wanna play."

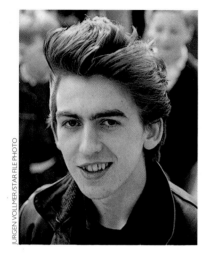

JÜRGEN VOLLMER/STAR FILE PHOTO

GEORGE

"I'm really quite simple," he assured us in his 1979 memoir, *I Me Mine*. "I don't want to be in the [music] business full-time because I'm a gardener. I plant flowers and watch them grow. I stay at home and watch the river flow." As we might've guessed when we heard that sitar, the quiet Beatle was destined to grow into the mystic Beatle, whose karma leads him to causes and calm. But if George's life is simple, it is nonetheless ambitious. In the early '70s he grew "tired of people saying, 'But what can I do?'" and organized the hugely successful benefit concerts for Bangladesh. His spiritual quest, nourished by his Hinduism, continues to involve him daily: "If there is a God, I want to see him, and Krishna consciousness and meditation are methods where you can actually see God and hear him, play with him." The flip side of this is George's keen sense of humor, still intact. He even cameoed in Eric Idle's 1978 film, *All You Need Is Cash,* about a rock band called the Rutles—the "Prefab Four." The parody, says George, told the Beatles' story "much better than the usual boring documentary," and the opportunity to laugh at his

Guitars were his sole obsession
when the group began. Today
there's more that stirs his soul.

WILLIAM COUPON

HULTON DEUTSCH

own past was wonderfully cathartic, an "escape into happiness." Indeed, it was so much fun that he put $11 million into the hilarious and irreverent *Life of Brian* and, later, started HandMade Films, helping to rejuvenate the British film industry (features included *Time Bandits, The Missionary* and *The Long Good Friday*). Of course, his life hasn't all been creativity and contemplation. One of the low points came in 1976, when he was found guilty of unconsciously plagiarizing the Chiffons' "He's So Fine" on "My Sweet Lord" and ordered to pay over a half million dollars in damages. But all things must pass. "I wouldn't say *anything* bothers him," his friend and fellow-guitarist Dave Edmunds marveled a decade later. "He's quite content with everything." Indeed, the elements of his contentment, at 53, are surprisingly diverse. Music (he sometimes joins pop luminaries Bob Dylan and Tom Petty in a group called the Traveling Wilburys), laughter, God and…auto racing. He's a big fan. "Those drivers have to be so together in their consciousness," he says. See? He's really quite simple.

"It's good to boogie once in a while," says George, with Hare Krishnas about the time of the breakup, and solo two decades later. "But when you boogie all your life away, it's just a waste."

GERED MANKOWITZ/LGI

"Ballads and babies," he says. "That's what happened to me." People complain that his post-Beatle music is too often sentimental, even treacly. "Tough," is his reply. If Paul is partial to "Silly Love Songs," it's no wonder: He is a very happy man. His happiness has, in 30-odd years, swung from the adolescent fantasy of Beatlehood ("I came into this to get out of having a job and to pull birds," he remembers, "and I pulled quite a few") to the kind of satisfaction that comes from a stable family life with his wife, Linda, and four children. "It's certainly not been as idyllic as it looks," he protests. "The bottom line is that we love each other, and what's more, we like each other. It sounds corny, but what else can I say?"

Nearly everything he has done since going out on his own has been touched by domesticity, beginning in 1971 when he found himself sitting in a green apron "praying like mad" over the birth of his third child and "the name 'Wings' just

ARCHIVE PHOTOS

As a teen dream, Paul seemed forever young, but since the Beatles' stormy breakup, he's become rock's best-loved elder statesman.

LINDA MCCARTNEY

came into my mind." The child was named Stella; he gave his new band the other name, and six years later the group shattered U.K. sales records with the single "Mull of Kintyre."

In 1991, with the debut of his *Liverpool Oratorio,* a classical homage to the city of his birth, he found a whole new audience. Critics called it "rousing" and "inspiring." Such respectability may be hard for some of his fans to accept, but Paul relishes the irony: "Heather, my eldest daughter, went out with Billy Idol. Just what a father needs. . . . Dear me!" But there is no indication he will be trading his bass for a pipe and slippers anytime soon. "I know the Beatles used to say, 'We won't be rock and rollin' when we're forty,' but I still love it." Forty? Try 53. "Bloody hell! That makes me old. So use me as a gauge and have a good time, and thank you very much for noticing me."

Domestic harmony and musical merriment are the instruments of Paul's pleasure.

John Lennon's songs endure because their message is timeless, simple and profound. "Make your own dream," he told us. "That's the Beatles' story, isn't it? I can't cure you. *You* can cure you." That's why there is no point in looking for his legacy in Yoko's cryptic art or his son Julian's pop songs or his son Sean's new band, the Pits, which made its debut in 1995 in a tavern in Oneonta, N.Y. (Sean, 20, wore a dress for that occasion.) Nor is there any point in looking for it in the countless cover versions that have been done of his work, be they ever so reverent. Fifteen years after his death, an extraordinarily diverse selection of pop stars—from Mary Chapin Carpenter to George Clinton to the Red Hot Chili Peppers—came together for a tribute album called *Working Class Hero*. Each artist sang one of John's songs, and all the perfor-

Some saw him as a working-class hero, others as a brilliant artist, but John Lennon never tried to be anything but himself.

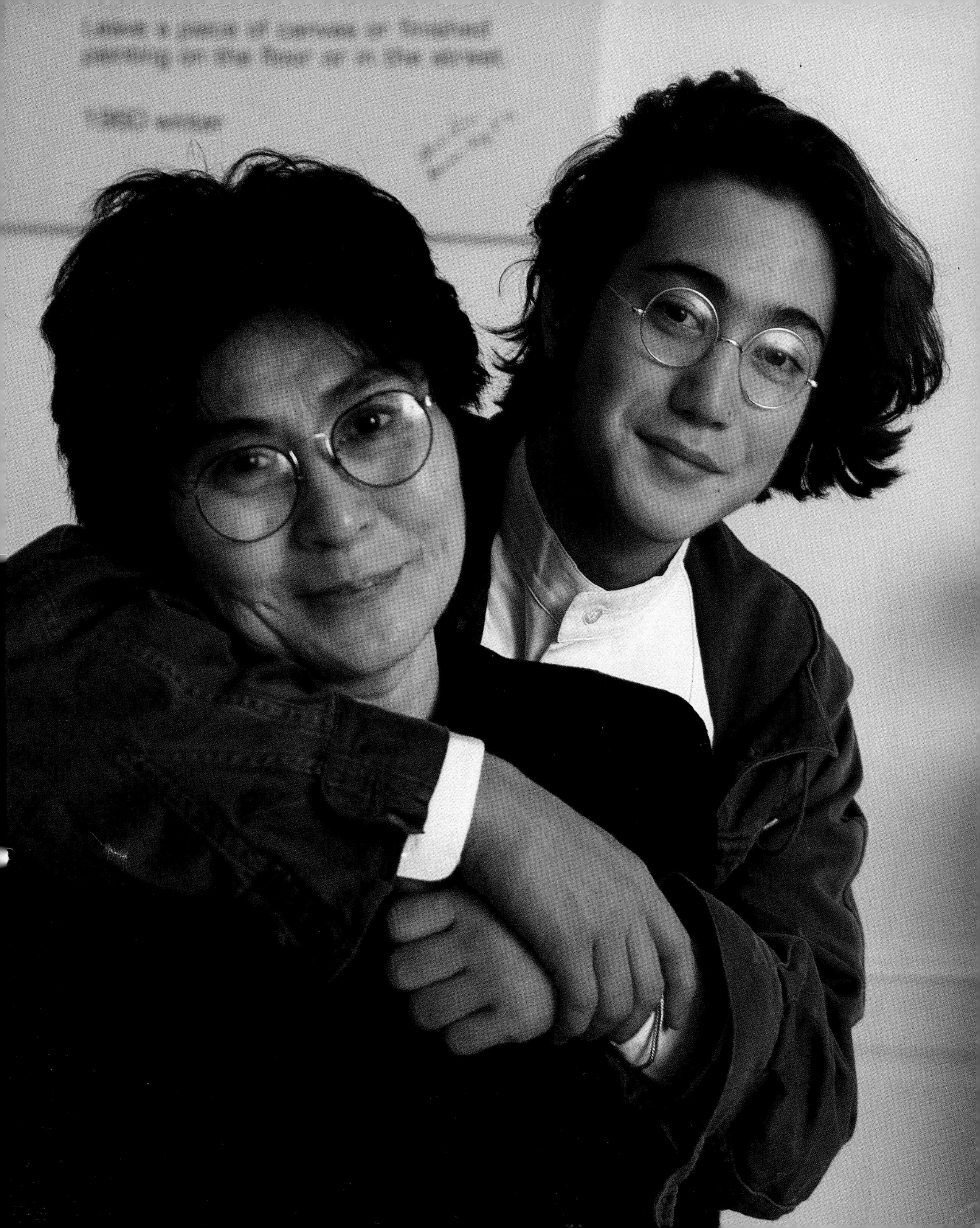

TWENTY-FIVE YEARS AFTER THE BREAKUP, RINGO, GEORGE

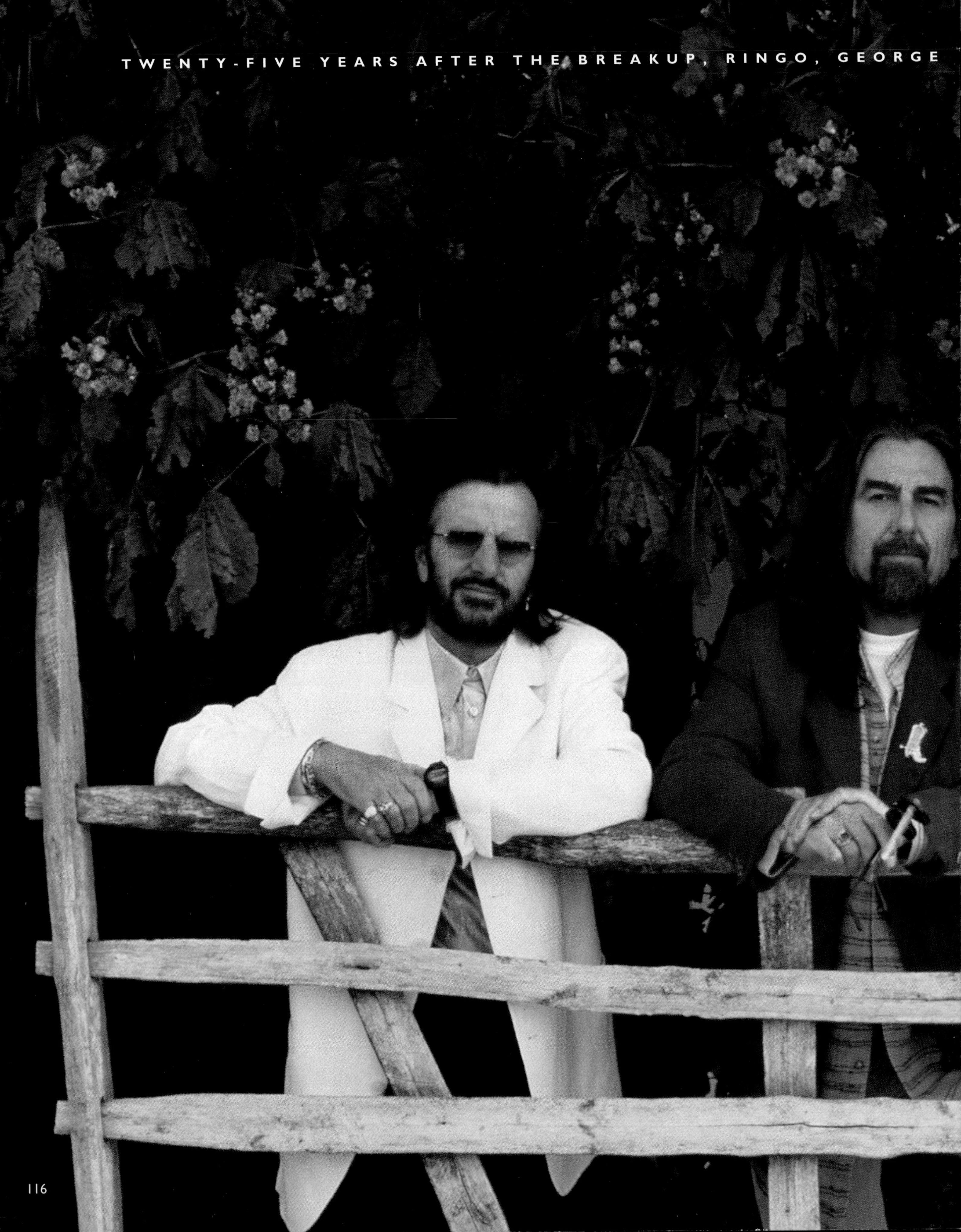

AND PAUL COME TOGETHER TO MAKE MUSIC AGAIN.

Imagine

Imagine the places of your life—your child-

hood home, your teenage haunts, the city where you first fell in love—turned into pub-

lic monuments on a connect-the-dots tourist map. If you were a Beatle, this would be

your strange reality. Now imagine there are no hordes of fans: no Beatle tours in Liver-

pool, no Letterman show in the Ed Sullivan Theater, no out-of-towners replicating the

famous walk across Abbey Road. Photographer Shimon Attie went to four places that

defined the Beatles. Some he found unchanged, others transformed by time. By captur-

ing, in a single frame, old images projected onto modern streetscapes, Attie created

these haunting portraits of homecoming and loss. He brought the Beatles back.

by Allison Adato
photography by Shimon Attie

L I V E R P O O L

The Cavern Club where the pre-Ringo Beatles reigned is gone. But a replica was built under the slope-roofed building behind this barren lot, and the neighborhood is still a center of nightlife. If Liverpool reminds the world of the Beatles, it has always reminded the Beatles of childhood: Paul of Penny Lane, John of Strawberry Field, George of his home at 12 Arnold Grove. "It was O.K., that house, very pleasant for being little. The worst was going to the big grammar school. That was when the darkness began, and I realized it was raining and clouding with old streets and backward teachers." But still: "Good place to wash your hair, Liverpool. Nice soft water."

H A M B U R G

"I was raised in Liverpool, but I grew up in Hamburg," John once said. Specifically the Reeperbahn, which was in 1960, as it is today, a stretch of clubs, strip joints and prostitution, a neon Gomorrah. The Beatles (with Pete Best and Stu Sutcliffe) led a nocturnal life here, John recalled: "What with playing, drinking and birds, how could we find time to sleep?" They couldn't, so they lived off the buzz of "Prellys," diet pills supplied by a washroom attendant at the Kaiserkeller. "Tired?" said Paul. "We were dead whacked." But they grew as musicians: "We could experiment. We got great kicks seeing the audiences react to different gear."

L O N D O N

"I want to play the drums before the Queen Mother," young Ringo once said. "Anything wrong with that?" The path to realizing that ambition ultimately took the Beatles to London and through the doors of EMI's Abbey Road Studios for an audition with George Martin. Seven years, 12 LPs and countless all-nighters later, they named their last effort for the place that bore witness to their genius, their goofs, their fabulous fights. As if shouting from the rooftops to this town that had granted them the fame they so desperately sought, they gave their final concert high above Savile Row. Said John when it was all over, "I hope we passed the audition."

N E W Y O R K

The Ed Sullivan Theater was the Beatles' Ellis Island, and all America an opportunity to be seized. For John, this city became something more—home. The others chose to be squires of the English countryside, but John fought deportation to stay in New York. "It's what Paris was in the 1920s—the center of the art world," he said. "And Yoko and I want to be in the center. I've got a lot of friends here, and I even brought my own cash." He was amazed he could go out and not be bothered. Yoko recalled his going on about "the taxi drivers talking with a rough edge, the docks." One day he told her why he loved it so. "It's like going back to Liverpool."